A Cruelty Special to Our Species

Poems

Emily Jungmin Yoon

An Imprint of HarperCollins*Publishers*

HarperCollins books may be purchased for educational, business, or sales promotional use. For information, please email the Special Markets Department at SPsales@harpercollins.com.

A hardcover edition of this book was published in 2018 by Ecco, an imprint of HarperCollins Publishers.

FIRST ECCO PAPERBACK EDITION PUBLISHED 2019.

Designed by Suet Yee Chong

Library of Congress Cataloging-in-Publication Data has been applied for.

ISBN 978-0-06-284370-8

19 20 21 22 23 LSC 10 9 8 7 6 5 4 3 2 1

A Cruelty
Special to
Our Species

Contents

Acknowledgments

Some of the poems in this manuscript also appear in the chapbook *Ordinary Misfortunes* (Tupelo Press, July 2017). The individual poems originally appeared in the following publications, sometimes in earlier versions:

Apogee: "On the Day of the Gyeongju Earthquake, September 12, 2016"

Berkeley Poetry Review: "An Ordinary Misfortune" [She is girl . . .]

The Collagist: "Dream Devil"

Day One: "Fetish"

The Journal: "An Ordinary Misfortune" [There was a man . . .] and "Comfort"

The New Yorker: "Time, in Whales"

The New York Times Magazine: "Autopsy"

The Offing: "An Ordinary Misfortune" [Mine is the jam-packed train . . .] and "An Ordinary Misfortune" [Okamoto condoms . . .]

OmniVerse: "Foreigner," "Notes," and "To the Winter Apricot Blossom"

PEN Poetry Series: "The Transformation"

Pinwheel: "An Ordinary Misfortune" [Hunting ground . . .], "An Ordinary Misfortune" [News reports that . . .], and "An Ordinary Misfortune" [The trouble with trees . . .]

Ploughshares: "An Ordinary Misfortune" [She offered him head . . .] and "An Ordinary Misfortune" [What is pressing . . .]

Poetry: "American Dream," "Bell Theory," and "Say Grace"

Prelude: sections "Jin Kyung-paeng," "Kang Duk-kyung," and "Kim Sang-hi" from "Testimonies"

Rattle (Poets Respond): "Hello Miss Pretty Bitch"

Reservoir: "Between Autumn Equinox and Winter Solstice, Today"
(published as "Today")

Southern Humanities Review: "Fear"

Sugared Water: "My Grandmother Reminisces with Peaches"

Tinderbox Poetry Journal: "Let Us Part Like This" and "News"

Up the Staircase Quarterly: "Royal Azalea" and "Sometimes when I'm walking
on this street"

The Volta: "*Don't Touch Me*," "Hair," Obeli," and sections "Hwang Keum-ju,"
"Kim Soon-duk," "Kim Yoon-shim," and "Pak Kyung-soon" from
"Testimonies"

Zócalo Public Square: "Easily written poem"

The sections in "Testimonies" draw upon documentary materials in
Comfort Women Speak: Testimony by Sex Slaves of the Japanese Military, edited
by Sangmie Choi Schellstede (Holmes & Meier, 2000), in *True Stories of
the Korean Comfort Women*, edited by Keith Howard (Cassell, 1996), and
in *Silence Broken: Korean Comfort Women* by Dai Sil Kim-Gibson (Mid-
Prairie Books, 1999), used in combination with my own language. The
testimonies by Hwang Keum-ju, Jin Kyung-paeng, Kang Duk-kyung, Kim
Soon-duk, and Pak Kyung-soon were recorded in Seoul, November 2, 1994;
that by Kim Sang-hi, in Seoul, October 29, 1994; that by Kim Yoon-shim,
in Washington, D.C., September 30, 1996. The transcribed, translated,
and transliterated testimonies are all from *Comfort Women Speak*; the
transliterations of Korean proper nouns in "Testimonies" are as printed in
this source text.

"*Don't Touch Me*" draws upon material in *Don't Touch Me* by MacKinlay
Kantor (Bantam Books, 1951), used in combination with my own language.

I would like to give huge thanks to the above magazines and Tupelo Press for first housing my poems, my agent Jin Auh of the Wylie Agency for believing in my manuscript before it was *A Cruelty Special to Our Species*, and the entire team at Ecco Books—especially Dan Halpern, Gabriella Doob, and Martin Wilson, with whom I virtually tossed the manuscript back and forth—for working on this book with care and dedication. You all made my book dream come true.

Great affection and appreciation to the Poetry Foundation, Barbara Deming Memorial Fund, Inc., Association of Writers & Writing Programs, Aspen Words, Community of Writers at Squaw Valley, The Home School, Asian American Writers' Workshop, and New York University's Creative Writing Program for providing financial and artistic support and space. The encouragement and generosity not only truly pushed this book into existence, but also charged me with so much confidence. I am forever indebted.

Deepest gratitude to my brilliant teachers at NYU's MFA program: Kimiko Hahn, Yusef Komunyakaa, Eileen Myles, Sharon Olds, Deborah Landau, Rachel Zucker, and Charles Simic. Their mentorship and faith shaped my poetry and this book in ways too numerous to count. Love to all the wonderful people who were the biggest champions of my work and/or were my first readers: David Krolikoski, Christopher Soto (a.k.a. Loma), Wo Chan, Elliot Lâm, Susan Su, Sabine Schulz, Sohye Kim, Minna Lee, Will Carroll, Nic Wong (a.k.a. Zhou Sivan), Sandra H. Park, Irene Inyoung Lee, Carol Kyul Han, Michelle Youngjin Kim, Jane Chungyoon Kim, SeungYun Lee, Soren Stockman and his family, Sam Herschel Wein, Cornelius Eady, Kien Lam, Terence Young, Kenneth May, Jack Jung, Don Mee Choi, Gregory Djanikian, Lynn Levin, Srikanth (Chicu) Reddy, Michael Bourdaghs, and Kyeong-Hee Choi. All your guidance, humor, pep talks, jumping jacks, tears, tender gazes at my readings, and shouts from rooftops for my poems energized and emboldened me.

Now I'd like to give a shout-out to my family, my pillar: my mother, Moonju Park, my father, Chulhyun Yoon, and my sister, Susan Kyungmin Yoon. Special thanks to my maternal grandmother, Sun-ja Yi, for telling the best stories and being my inspiration. 저의 첫 시작詩作의 시작始作부터 변함없이 저의 꿈을 아껴주시고 응원해주신 덕분에 여기까지 올 수 있었습니다. 이 책으로써 감사의 마음을 소소하고 詩詩하게나마 표현할 수 있게 되어 행복합니다. 고맙습니다. 사랑합니다.

Also, woof woof to my dogs, in heaven and on earth, who listened to all my secrets and heartbreaks and taught me a lot about love.

Finally, I am very grateful for you, reader. Thank you for meeting me here.

Author's Note

For me, poetry provides a space in which intertwined languages and historical narratives are celebrated—a space in which I conceive disasters, failures, and traumas, lending them my own perspective, dimension, and articulation. My poetry does not exist to answer, but rather to continue asking, questions about my immigrant, ESL, Korean, and womanly experiences, and the violent history of twentieth-century Korea.

As poems on the "comfort women" of the Japanese Empire are in the heart of this collection, I'd like to mention my position in writing their stories. In 1991, the year of my birth, Kim Hak-sun became the first former "comfort woman" to offer public testimony of her life as a sex slave. As more and more former "comfort women" of the Japanese Empire began to share their testimonies, it was clear: they were speaking from within, not for, a community. They put their voices together for reparations and recognition of their, and the Empire's, history. I'd like my poetry to serve to amplify and speak these women's stories, not speak *for* them. I'd like my poetry to remind readers that even if a part of history may not seem to be relevant to their lives, it is—it is their reality too. An experience that is not mine is still part of the society and world that I occupy. It is crucial to know, listen, tell, and retell various stories, so we may better theorize and understand our existence.

In the realm of poetry, one can transcend the sense of belonging confined by temporal and geographical lines. In this transcendence, I return to my departed ancestors—to their frustration of tongues and identities, and experiences of diaspora—from the Japanese occupation to the turbulent years in Korea before my birth. Poetry is not just relief; poetry is tension. Poetry is departure. Poetry is return. Poetry is memory. I wrote this book to say that one has the agency to command and preserve their own narrative.

The Charge

An Ordinary Misfortune

Mine is the jam-packed train. The too-weak cocktail. This statement by an American man at the bar: *Your life in Korea would have been a whole lot different without the US.* Meaning: be thankful. This question by a Canadian girl, a friend: *Why don't you guys just get along?* The guys: Japan and Korea. Meaning: move on. How do I answer that? Move on, move on, girls on the train. Destination: comfort stations. Things a soldier can do: mount you before another soldier is done. Say, *Drink this soup made of human blood.* Say, *The Korean race should be erased from this earth.* Tops down. Bottoms up. Things erased: your name, your child, your history. Your new name: Fumiko, Hanako, Yoshiko. Name of the condom: Charge Number One. Name of the needle: Compound 606. Salvarsan means, an arsenic to save. Ratio 291: 29 soldiers per girl. Actual count: lost. Lost: all. Shot, shot, shot, everybody. Give thanks.

Comfort

On Wednesday, I ate plain yogurt.
 Opened a notebook. Vivaldi
as I folded my laundry.

It was his birthday. On Wednesday,
 it rained. On the succulents,
on the surviving women.

Tricked or taken, carted to Japanese soldiers.
 The condom said *Attack Number One*.
Rinsed for reuse. On Wednesday,

I listened to The Four Seasons.
 It stopped raining. It never stopped
raining. On Wednesdays, it rains

for the children they bore. For the children
 they could not bear. For the children
they were. Give them this day. Give them

Vivaldi, violin, give them the all-girls choir.
 L'inverno, come and gone. All four seasons,
come and gone. On Wednesday,

nothing happened. Rain evaporated,
 and so did the concertos.
Wednesdays ago, the women,

the girls, clutched each other. Who will live,
who will leave, who believes this life.
The world will be better after you and me.

An Ordinary Misfortune

What is pressing. What is pressed. Or who. My grandmother. A woman. A teen. Her father presses the gates shut. Presses her into a crate. The crate into a shed. She unfolds by morning. Binds her chest. She walks unwomanned. An American soldier sees her and yells *Stop over there!* in Japanese. The language they've both learned. When she runs, she is unmistakably woman. She falls. He laughs. What is a body in a stolen country. Or whose. What is right in war. What is left in war. War hasn't left Korea. I have. I fold. I give up, myself, to you. Which one of you said *Let's have raunchy Korean sex* to me. Which one of you didn't. Do you represent America to me. Did those soldiers to her. *We didn't fear war. We feared the allies,* she said.

Hello Miss Pretty Bitch

the street drummer

calls out in Korean

no doubt thinking it

a compliment

a pleasant surprise

cinched with red ribbons

for Christmas the day

select theatres will gift us

with *The Interview*

a comedy in which

two American journalists

ignite Kim Jong-un's face

freedom has prevailed

the film's star Seth Rogen

says about the release

the same was thought

at the time of Korea's release

from the Japanese Empire

though then the Korean War

began and compared to war

what's so bad about a movie

anyway even war can be funny

and now a drummer

in New York says

you got a smile

that could light up

the whole town

though I'm not smiling

thinking about villages

and cities of what became

North Korea set on fire

sending puddles of twilight

into sunless skies

as if flames could stab

but his freedom

of speech prevails

freedom always prevails

which is why we get to see

two Americans

incinerate a Korean face

on Christmas

hold our popcorn

and chocolate bars

and laugh as the dictator

explodes in tune

to a pop song

laugh as American

soldiers would laugh

at Korean children

chanting *hello hello*

gibu me choco-let

with wartime hunger

laugh as they choose

which face

to light up

An Ordinary Misfortune

The trouble with trees is that their bodies and limbs are too capable, capable of burning, of living, capable of leaves, of leaving, charcoal, ash, and we think we have power. *Capable*, 1561, from Late Latin *capabilis* "receptive," Unit 731 of the Japanese Empire injects us with monkey blood, our limbs are not receptive, *Capable*, used by theologians, from Latin *capax* "able to hold much," our living bodies and extracted children, not holding, not *Capable*, *capere* "to take, grasp, lay hold, catch, undertake, be large enough for, comprehend," how to take, how to grasp, comprehend, our limbs catch fire, taken, our bodies not large enough, *Capable*, Sanskrit *kapati* "two handfuls," two handfuls of intestines, are they *Capable*, Greek *kaptein* "to swallow, gulp down," pills, gas, what more, *Capable*, Lettish *kampiu* "seize," our limber bodies, carve our bodies, our eyes unseized by their sockets, *Capable*, limbs, capable of burning, of ash, charcoal, *Capable*, Old Irish *cacht* "servant girl," her fallopian tube, cut, living, not *Capable*, of living, leaving, Welsh *caeth* "captive, slave," *Capable*, our names, *maruta*, from Japanese, "logs."

An Ordinary Misfortune

She is girl. She is gravel. She is grabbed. She is grabbed like handfuls of gravel.
Gravel grated by water. Her village is full of gravel fields. It is 1950. She is girl.
She is grabbed. She is not my grandmother, though my grandmother is girl.
My grandmother's father closes the gates. Against American soldiers, though
they jump over stone walls. To a girl who is not my grandmother. The girl is
gravel grabbed. Her language is gravel because it means nothing. Hands full
of girl. Fields full of gravel. Korea is gravel and graves. Girl is girl and she will
never be a grandmother. She will be girl, girl is gravel and history will skip her
like stone over water. Oh girl, oh glory. Girl.

The Testimonies

Testimonies

Hwang Keum-ju

a draft notice for girls, who was going to go? Everybody
crying. I went. I dressed nicely and went
 train windows covered with tar paper
None of the girls knew
 Japanese soldiers on horses vast Manchurian field
It was now much too cold to sleep
thanks to our body warmth, the sun rose
 I waited for them to send me to a factory
They could not possibly dump me here
 I was called Nagaki Haruko
 My long hair was still braided
An officer told me that there were five orders to obey
 If I missed any I would be less than dead
I hoped one of the orders was for me to work at a factory.
 I looked at his jacket hung inside out to hide his name
I looked at my virgin's braid at his knife He told me
 I was not going to any factory
told me to take off my clothes I told him
I did not understand his order
and his kind of factory and he laughed
 Girls arrived got sick pregnant injected
with so many drugs nameless animals
exploded on top of us
The day of liberation Suddenly,
no sound of horses the last soldier
stood in the kitchen "Your country is liberated,
 and my country is sitting on a fire."

So I left the barracks
　　　I walked
I was alone and walked all the way to the 38th parallel
American soldiers sprayed me with so much DDT
　　　all the lice fell off me
It was December 2nd
I lost my uterus
　　　I am now 73 years old.

Jin Kyung-paeng

my mother and I were picking cotton
when two Japanese *Kempei* passed by
 she told me to lie flat
But they found me
kicked my mother
 put me aboard a ship then a bigger ship
which arrived near Kinariyama, Taiwan
 a place with many monkeys and snakes
 potatoes, sweet potatoes, taro
50 women were not enough for these soldiers
I remember a few of them Kanemoto Hideo
 He treated us okay also
Oono Nakamura, Yoshida Kanjiro
 Yamaguchi Higashi Inamochi
I stayed with them until
 the end of war One day in August
 the soldiers gathered and wept
In March, we sailed to Pusan
 An American GI gave me a bag of candy and 1,000 *won*
We bought rice
 a good meal
I was *wianbu* between 14 and 19
I became feverish I became infertile
I remember the children of my dead husband
I remember a good meal I am alone
I looked like a stranger at home in Hapchon with my darkened skin
 my mother thought she was dreaming

Kang Duk-kyung

my school teacher asked me if I wanted
 to go to Japan do something good for the Emperor
we were led to a harbor
a cargo ship a train
 to a factory in Doyamaki where
Food was so scarce we pulled grass, roots anything we could eat
girls died of hunger some went crazy
I ran away was found by a Japanese soldier
 Kobayashi
 took me
 to a hut Every evening
 soldiers
countless soldiers on the wild mountainside
 Kobayashi
An unusually quiet day
 I found Japan had lost the war
I sailed to Korea
jumped from the crates hit my stomach with fists
I failed I named him Young-ju
 left him at an orphanage
met him every Sunday
 one Sunday
I saw another boy in his clothes
Young-ju had died of pneumonia
 already buried
I thought of Kobayashi bringing me rice
in his drunken stupor I thought of the piece of steel
I took at the factory

I found some of the steel so attractive
I still believe he is alive
somewhere I want to believe
that all was just a terrible fate
But then,
 But then

Kim Sang-hi

I was 14 years old It was around November 26th
 It snowed, I remember. I was on my way home
from the photo-studio with my portrait when a man in olive-drab clothing
grabbed me by the collar cursed in Japanese was he Japanese
 or Korean I could not tell
I was thrown onto a truck of mournful sounds of weeping
 these girls and I crossed the border into China
there was no poison no ropes
In Suzhou I was #4 I was Takeda Sanai
 The first night an officer grabbed me
I drank disinfectant
 but I didn't die
In Nanjing I had malaria
 appendicitis hemorrhage in my vagina
 but I didn't die
In Singapore I saw dark-skinned men digging ditches
 they looked at us as if they would burst into tears
In Singapore the war ended
 we boiled leaves from trees and wild greens
 we ate this to survive
When I made it back to Pusan Harbor
 I went to my brother's house in Taegu
in his dream: I had shaved my head was drowning in the ocean
 but I didn't die
My name is Kim Sang-hi
I was born on December 20, 1920
I was born into a good family
I am a Catholic

I should forget and forgive	but I cannot
When my head turns toward Japan	I curse her
I want to find solace	but I cannot
When I wake up every morning	I cannot

Kim Yoon-shim

An automobile drove up the road, something I had never seen
before. The driver let me climb up and the truck rolled on
 then kept on going
 and going and I begged them
to take me back but I was thrown
 into a cargo train a cargo ship Harbin
 a comfort station where three truckloads
of soldiers arrived One by one they raped all
night long with filthy wordless bodies
 my child's body
they impregnated girls and still forced sex
When a child was born
 a blue-uniformed woman put the body
 in a sack and carried it away
soldiers used the "sack": *saku*
 reused condoms girls got sick
 When a girl got too sick
 a guard wrapped her body
 in a blanket and carried her away
Such was our life
 look at my fingers
 when I ran away the police smashed my hands
weaving a stiff pen between my fingers
 like this.
Another year passed
 like this.
 In June 1945
 when the camp seemed deserted

 I escaped and ran all night
in a month I reached Korean shores
 In Harbin, I saw at a stream a hand
of a sick girl
who had been buried alive.
 In my dreams, she is still reaching
 toward wider waters
 my hands with their crooked fingers
cannot help her

Pak Kyung-soon

There was a man about 45 years of age with a mustache
 who told me to work for Japan
 and meet my brother in Hiroshima
The man said my refusal might not be good for my parents
 The man and his men took me to Shimonoseki
 I was led into a room I was told to take a bath I was told
 to take off my clothes
I only begged that I meet my brother
 When they finally took me to Hiroshima, my brother was alone
 in a big, empty room he asked if I came
 as a "comfort woman" and I promised
 I would return
 to see him again
When flower buds were about to appear
I was taken to Osaka In its room
 I was Number 10 I was then
a "comfort woman"
 I became so sick with syphilis I could not walk
One night an officer came and told me to get ready
I was in such great pain the next thing I remember
 is arriving in Seoul It was June 1945
 Immediately I had a miscarriage
The mustached man learned of my return
 told me to return to the "comfort station"
 To avoid the draft again I got married
our new life a rented room
 I could smell the odor of my weekly "#606"
 arsenic for syphilis

My baby discharged pus from his ears
 was called crazy
My brother returned home with burns and lumps
 all over his body from radiation
 discharged disintegrated bone
 the size of teeth near his wounds
The Japanese soldiers discharged
 discharge out of charge into
 every room

Kim Soon-duk

there was "girl delivery" just like
 farmers' mandatory delivery
 of harvested rice
to the government. I wanted to hide
 but what if my mother was captured
 in my place
My mother was needed at home Mother
Mother I decided to go
 they promised a job as a military nurse in Japan
Mother a man gathered us near the county office
 and took us to Pusan to Nagasaki
That night the girl next to me went missing
Each night they sent several virgin girls to military officers
 a military officer came to me and said
 every young girl experiences sex in her lifetime
 that I might as well do it now
they took us they took us to Shanghai to a ruined village
 my body a ruined village a damaged house
our manager gave me packets of black powder
 to reduce my bleeding from the vagina
He then told me it was made
 from a leg
 of a Chinese soldier's corpse
 I dream of human legs rolling around I dream it
 to this day
I scream to wake myself up Mother Izumi
 he was kind to me I told him about my thoughts of suicide

He was surprised so surprised

 he sent me home sent me letters

 I did not reply. I had my new life to live:

as a washerwoman, a street peddler and I did other things too

 but Mother the hardest time was when I was dreaming

 of suicide

 while soldiers were standing in line to satisfy their lust

 in the ruined village

when I was dreaming of legs that could not go anywhere.

The Confessions

An Ordinary Misfortune

Hunting ground with knife-ghosts. Clubbed raw. My body, ground down. You'd think a former comfort woman would hate the Japanese. I don't. I hate men and I hate sex. I hate the sight of my son-in-law, who lives in this house. I've been living a robbed house. My room became unfit for children. How could I put a child in a haunted place. Nothing can grow in this blubber and blood. My husband found lovers somewhere else. I found my daughters somewhere else. I love them with the longing of a house no one occupies. They sometimes put their hands on its creaking walls and say, *What's wrong? What's wrong?* Every door is closed. 70 years and no one knows. No one who knows my past is alive. Girls at the comfort stations, we were all children then.

Fetish

Let me tell a Korean joke.
A woman puts on her white clothes for mourning
and goes to a wake. She wails for hours, then asks,
So who died? I think about this woman

and her performance of grief. The essential grief.
Colonial-era Japanese historians were sure
the white pottery and clothes of Korea show perpetual
sorrow. Poverty of color, incapacity for pleasure—

countless foreign invasions turned the people blank
and hollow, cursed to eternal mourning.
Those historians spoke pity for the peninsularians
and their endearing purity of a spotless vase.

But perhaps that joke is funny because the woman
feels no grief. Perhaps she is a moirologist, which means
professional mourner, but sounds more like some kind of
scientist. Perhaps she is both, her research field, sorrow.

Royal Azalea

My friend. You can't tell me apart
from my sister, my cousin. My friend.
 You want to pluck away
at my gut. Digest my origins, crush me
with your teeth.
There are mountains of me.
Fluorescent, inflorescent.
 Infrared: mountains of us.
Find me with azalea. Confuse me
 with azalea.
Find constellations where I open.
 Royal flush
 of my skin: you've found
my nectar guide.
 Touch me underneath
my regalia, I'm viscid.
Taste me, I'm sweet. You won't even know
the toxin on your tongue,
 in your gut now.

Don't Touch Me

MacKinlay Kantor's 1951 novel is *savagely outspoken*! Air Force men in Japan and wives of men transferred to the front. Wives are greedy. Hungry for men. Sing-song girls perch in the exotic gardens of Kumbawa, the exotic backwash of the Korean War.

*

Konnichiwa, a street vendor tries me in a sing-song voice. What, no *ni hao* this time? I would have said, if I were more outspoken. I could be Japanese. An exotic backwash.

*

MacKinlay, lend me your words: I could be a garden. Awaiting the Male. To whom the Male came seldom. Who sings with a thin voice, bits of lace that flash beneath the hems, wonderful female things. To whom the Male is the carrier-arounder, the thrower-arounder. Who is the receptacle. That goes back to the caves. Maybe past. Oh, I would smell of Asia. A Geisha-Schmeisha. I might be horizontal. Little things, pretty things, the gilt shelves of rare teacups, the inlaid coffee table with its carvings. A fresh new spice to taste. Touch and taste. Fruit and flowers. Spice and incense. Cloudy breath amid my draperies, emanating from my strange other-worldly body. I could be this. Greedy and hungry for men. Singing songs of my conquerors. Savage.

*

"Kumbawa," "syanata"? Mac, they're not even said right. *Konnichiwa,* on the other hand, is.
"Ah so desska," you say.

*

Man, you want to explore sex as practiced among the *Japanese*. I would smell of Asia. Spice and incense. You think, *I should know the silky menace of your touch, the violence of your gasping effort, the shudder of fulfillment, the invocation growled in your throat when explosion wracks you. Without that, I am incomplete.* You think that without you, I'd be incomplete. Conqueror. Carrier-arounder. Thrower-arounder.

*

Tell it to him straight, Mac: mingling your body with that of a *Japanese woman*, flesh against flesh, fluid touching fluid, you violate yourself. This race! Raw fish, polluted pickles. Toilers, gesticulating shopkeepers, pitiful elders, men and women knobbed and bony. Skimpy hair twisted to a horror. I would smell of Asia. Man, my race oozes from bamboo and other thatching. Goes back to the cave.

*

A man brings the needle to the thread, a woman brings the thread to the needle. Maybe there's something phallic about that. Okay, Mac. If I were an exotic garden of needles,
I'd let you touch me.

*

I'm being as honest as a woman can.

Bell Theory

When I was laughed at for my clumsy English, I touched my throat.
Which said *ear* when my ear said *year* and year after year
I pronounced a new thing wrong and other throats laughed.
Elevator. Library. Vibrating bells in their mouths.

How to say *azalea*. How to say *forsythia*.
Say instead golden bells. Say *I'm in ESL.* In French class
a boy whose last name is Kring called me *belle.*
Called me by my Korean name, pronouncing it wrong.
Called it loudly, called attention to my alien.

(I touched the globe moving in my throat, a hemisphere sinking.)

Called me across the field lined with golden bells.
I wanted to run and be loved at the same time. By Kring.
As in ring of people. *Where are you going? We're laughing* with *you.*

The bell in our throat that rings with laughter is called uvula. From *uva*: grape.
A theory: special to our species, this grape-bell has to do with speech.
Which separates us from animals. Kring looked at me and said
Just curious, do you eat dogs? and I wanted to end my small life.
Be reborn a golden retriever of North America.
Lie on a field lined with golden bells, loved.

Today, in a country where dogs are more cherished
than a foreign child, an Oregon Senate candidate says no
to refugees. Says, years ago, Vietnamese refugees ate dogs,
harvested other people's pets. *Harvest* as in *harvest* grapes.

Harvest as in *harvest* a field of golden rice. As do people
from rice countries. As in people-eat-dog worlds.

Years ago, 1923 Japan, the phrase *jūgoen gojissen* is used
to set apart Koreans: say 15 *yen* 50 *sen*. The colonized who use the chaos
of the Kanto Earthquake to poison waters, set fire: a cruelty special to
 our species.
A cruelty special to our species—how to say *jūgo*, how to say *gojit*,
how *jūgo* sounds like die in Korean, how *gojit* sounds like lie—
lie, lie, library, azalea, library.

I'm going to the library, I lied, years ago, on a field lined with forsythia.

American Dream

The alcove of your arm
has become my favorite room
for sleep, but I've been roused
by nightmares lately. *Even thunderstorms
couldn't wake you,* my mother says
over the phone. I want to tell her
I've been seeing a white man, an American
man, but I can already imagine her:
Well, you can have friends. She had never meant
for me to become a Westerner—
she's afraid of losing me to a *foreigner,* being unable to speak
to her future grandchildren. Thousands of miles away
in Korea she asks if anything is wrong. I want to laugh.
Say to you, *Isn't she ridiculous?* But
last night a Korean man broke into your room
and raped me, with you calm in your repose
next to me. He sat on my stomach with a knife,
the only gleaming thing. And you were still
in your platinum skin when I opened my eyes. *How
can anything be wrong,* I comfort my mother.

Hair

My mother would straighten then wind the cord
of the hair dryer around its oblong trunk,
its mouth curving out to a flat triangle like a delta,
after it has done its duty of releasing streams of strong air
for our heads, then said, *See? We have to keep neat*
everywhere. At the age of six, when I started drying
my own hair, the dryer was heavy and unwieldy in my hands,
so often my head was patches of dry and wet,
but I would wrap the dryer with its cord carefully and
with precision, unlooping any bump to coil again,
admiring how the tight spiral with its consistent shine looked
indeed like perfect wet hair. It wasn't until my early twenties
my hair started to curl on its own, and my mother said,
My world! Your hair is turning into your father's! How peculiar is it
that when I wanted wavy hair as an adolescent, to be more
like the white girls I cherished, my hair was obstinately perpendicular
to the earth. How peculiar is it that these girls
would stroke my long dark hair and told it how so smooth &
lovely it is. Fetishization I welcomed for long.
Summer days and the popular girl saying *I would kill*
for your skin tone, my mother's friends whispering to her,
Why did Jungmin tan so much, like I have a reason
for being a color at some place and at some time
and there is a straight line between bad and goodness
on which I lay my unbeautiful body precariously.
Autumn morning. Leaves begin to split and crimp in the cold,
& holding the dryer, I still do this slow meandering.

Obeli

How fitting the obelus
dotted the margins of ancient manuscripts,
marking spurious passages, then became the symbol
for division, one line balancing a circle above
and a circle beneath, two heads never to touch
each other. How our peninsula became one
obelus. How swift the sunderance
of families. How fitting that division
is military. In elementary school, we learned
division, its quotient and remainder, sang
about reunification, brought bags of rice
for our northern half, not knowing
the spurious passages they would travel,
that the white grains never touched the hands
we held in our paintings. How enduring the sunderance
of lovers. How the obelus gets its name from a spit,
a lance, how in college my Korean boyfriend registered
to fulfill the compulsory military service, how
his American friends joked about killing all the North
Koreans, beheading them, how when he laughed,
it was as though his shaved head was of
somebody else. How I thought about reunification again,
wanted the armistice to be over, to be brought
to swift justice for my sake.

My Grandmother Reminisces
with Peaches

Peaches you eat at night.
In the dark you can't see the insect bites.
How do they find the sweetest fruit?

Your grandfather would find it—the one
unblemished peach in someone's orchard—
and cool it in the stream for me.
I married him that year.

He wasn't a romantic, you know.
But he always left a basket of peaches
at my feet in the summer.
I carved pieces of that viscous fruit
and placed them on the parted lips
of my sleeping children. And they rose
chewing on the pulp.

Look at how my garden balsam has bloomed.
Dye your fingers with its petals—see if it lasts till first snow.
Snow, what precious flower in this region.
With my ear resting on his chest, I could imagine its blossom.

My cheek dreamt well on his heart.

An Ordinary Misfortune

There was a man. A Japanese soldier. One that did not believe in old superstitions. One that did not believe in sex before battle as charm against harm. He was an odd man. One that did not carry an amulet with pubic hair of a comfort woman. Or any piece of her. His comrades said, *Be a man.* The equation is, an odd man out is not a man. There is no reason for logic in war. There is no reason. There was a man. His comrades said, *Come raid, come pillage.* Pushed him into the station. Their eyes on the holes in the wall. Watched as he came. Became. What is the equation here. There is a no equation here. There was a man. One who said weeping, *I am not a man, I am not a man.*

Autopsy

Your fingers crowned with meat hooks and cleavers.
You holding me and whispering, *Who did this to you?*
sawing me into a shallow boat.
You did, you did, you did, and you, and you, and you,
you did this to me in my home, you did this while crying.
I cannot make a sound as though my mouth is full
of honey. Of a colony of bees. Honey, honey.
You lift my skin. Inside it lives your dream of forests
where snow grows old and you are young,
cold and white and lonely
without my suffering, and you want to say, *Not me,*
not me, I wouldn't hurt a bee,
but honey. Inside my blood and bone
and their network of tendon and meat we have,
you and I, our histories of hunting
and being the beast. If not,
what are we doing here, my dead body
and you, assessing my death,
looking at your hands like a fool,
like a child who finds that a dandelion will die
only after he has plucked it?

The After

An Ordinary Misfortune

Okamoto condoms are number one in Korea. The 001 series. The 002, 003. The thinnest. The pinnacle of condom technology. The pinnacle of pleasure. A wonder. No wonder. Who wouldn't want that. On Okamoto's website: SKINLESS SKIN: a popular condom since postwar (which war?). No mention of Totsugeki Ichiban: meaning: Charge Number One, Assault Number One, Attack Number One, Attack Champion, Attack and Blast, choose your own definition. Who wore it? Who wore it best? In comfort stations, there weren't enough Number Ones. Attack and Blast, rinse, attack and blast, repeat. The girls' skinless skin. Blasted, postwar (which war?): *gyokusai*: meaning: "shattered jade": better a broken jewel than an unbroken tile: honorable death: erase any evidence: the girls' skinless skin. Blast more holes into their bodies. 000.

An Ordinary Misfortune

She offered him head because he wanted her whole. *You could at least blow me,* he offered. She didn't want to offend. He was taking his pants off. *Are we on?* he said. She was in love. She said *I'm in.* When she couldn't finish him off, he was put off. She should've put out. Because *Look what you did,* he said. *Look what you did. That wasn't even worth it.* He felt blue. She felt bad. She sucked. She blew it. She remembered Googling *putting out* and finding: *Chris lost interest in Ashley because she wasn't putting out. Joe dumped his girlfriend because she won't "put out" for him. If a gal doesn't "put out" by the third date, I dump her.* Something was off. *Guys are like that, though, guys need it more,* she had been offered. It's her fault if she turns him on, doesn't get him off. If he wanted her whole. If he left. *Whore. Girls always use sex to get what they want,* someone had cracked. The teacher was showing versions of *Judith with the Head of Holofernes.* Klimt. Caravaggio. Gentileschi. Allori. She remembered Allori. Judith looking out at her. Holding the head by the hair. As if to offer. To allure.

Fear

I wanted to carve it out of me—
become a fjord flanked
by historic cliffs. How else
could I write the years
I did not live. I wanted the space
for fear emptied, teem with lives
like the black-and-white photos
of Max Desfor's.
I don't know what I expected to feel
in front of his Korean War photograph.
The image that won him the Pulitzer
held refugees crawling a wrecked bridge,
but this wasn't it—
it was a pair of hands,
blackened fingers sprouting out of snow
with a hole above them.
Desfor says, in a screen behind me,
"The man's hands were bound and that black hole
was where he breathed his last."
That black hole, that sphere
of fingers. That oceanic arm, that fjord
of mine. Holding what I had believed
to be void. Voice,
a fearful current. Underneath,
bodies of light,
of water.

Let Us Part Like This

On winter nights Koreans heard infant cries
from distant wood owls. An abandoned newborn
amidst black trees, unaware
that it may be a bird. Allow us
to be like that. Let us speak these words louder
than pines cracking in the snow. Walk far from us.
Mistake us for howling animals.
That's ten of them, that's a hundred of them that we left
behind. Maybe hundreds, maybe thousands.

News

For the victims of the MV Sewol disaster of April 16, 2014

There's an article on how to eat an apple.
　　But I am eating a pear and thinking
　　pear in Korean is a homonym for *ship* or *boat*
　　　　and *stomach,* how MV Sewol sank, how *sewol*
　　　　means *beyond the world* and homonymous with
　　　　the *passing time or life.* It carried mostly young students
　　　　on a school trip, told to wait in the stomach of Sewol while
　　　　the captain and crew fled. Divers pull bodies, find a boy and a girl
　　　　strapped together by life vests. Koreans wear yellow ribbons, unbury
　　　　the young dead from the salts of too-quick passing life. A letter pasted
　　　　on a bottle atop the walls of their high school reads: *I have loved you*
　　　　for a year. Sewol, how did I love at seventeen? Lull the clot
　　　　in my stomach? Watered with tears, the pit grew vines
　　　　around my veins, and I coughed petals. I surrendered
　　　　and cried, I love, I love! and lived. I am sick
　　of the smiling slices of pear. The right way to eat
an apple is: top to bottom, swallow everything. Waste nothing
except seeds. A homonym for *apple* is *apology.* I am sorry,
I say to the pear's core, to the seeds in the sunken belly.

An Ordinary Misfortune

News reports that in the Philippines, more Koreans than locals are killed. *Because of the gangs. Because Filipinos think Koreans are rich. Because Filipino laborers return from Korea with a bad taste in their mouths.* More "Korean Desks" in the police *for the safety of our people.* In other news, Korea leads in: tourists, businessmen, students looking for a guiltless fuck, guiltless departure, saying, *These Filipinas, these children can't find me.* Nothing but a bad taste in their mouths. Nothing but an emptied desk. In other news, two boys file a suit against their Korean father. Say, *Were you not in the Philippines with us for 7 years?* Say, *Won't you take a DNA test?* Do the same men read about comfort women and rage with all of us, keep bibles in their desks and preach, *Violence begets violence?* Curse aloud, *Damn Filipinos taking Korean lives?* The boys win the suit. Their father says, *This will break up my family.*

Notes

*Japan and S. Korea have an agreement on the "Comfort Women" issue,
December 28, 2015*

Pictures of two men shaking hands: Foreign Minister Kishida and Foreign Minister Yun.

The "Government of Japan confirms that this issue is resolved finally and irreversibly with this announcement."

(1 billion yen = $8.3 million US)

"The Government of the Republic of Korea acknowledges the fact that the Government of Japan is concerned about the [*Comfort Woman*] statue built in front of the Embassy of Japan in Seoul from the viewpoint of preventing any disturbance of the peace of the mission or impairment of its dignity."

Statue: Bronze. Hair ripped short. Short. Empty chair to her right (to remember the others). Small (is only a girl). Small feet on small toes (unable to tread with ease). *How can we sleep with feet stretched when . . .* (common Korean expression)

—also where former comfort women and citizens have gathered every Wednesday for the last 24 years (demanding peace, dignity) (yellow butterfly badges)

Video of Yi Yongsu, to junior foreign minister Im: Why are you trying to kill us twice? Did you exclude us because we're uneducated, too old? Because you think I don't know anything?

Will you live this life for me?

Wall Street Journal posts translated agreement. One person comments.

*S. Korea must realize that the offensive statues of the comfort woman have been and will be the symbol of S. Korean perjury and calumny. Comfort women dedicated to raise soldiers' morale and spirits, and to prevent rape crimes in countries.**

*(Rape to prevent rape, prevent disturbance of peace, impairment of dignity)

We used to believe butterflies pulled spring over the earth. How many springs now. Ask the deranged butterfly to dance—it will not.

(Average age of the surviving women: 90)

On the Day of the Gyeongju Earthquake,
September 12, 2016

All I want to think about is love and gratitude,
on the escalator in Busan Station, having put you on the train
back to Seoul, avoiding the eyes of the doomsayer on the staircase
next to my descending steps, as he screams death upon those
who don't accept God. The end is coming, so come to church.
Or the earth will split open to swallow you and you won't
be saved. He spits a different miracle on each face. God slits
the sea down the woman behind me. Flame bursts into the world
and water fills it, then overflows. It is not that I don't fear water
and fire. It is not that I don't believe in God. We already kill
and die with water and fire. An ocean away the police will shoot
Terence Crutcher then Keith Lamont Scott and it will not be the end
and here Baek Nam-gi will die from a water cannon and none of this
was for not believing in the right power, which is God.
The doomsayer says we must surrender and he is sure of this.
Across the station, windows of love motels light up then dim
as lovers enter the room, empty for, empty into each other.
The end of summer is coming. I have now walked far away
from the man. It is not that I don't believe in God. For once all I want is
to think about love and gratitude, thank God for all our lives.
When the earth begins to tremble, I look back to the station
already emptied of your train. No one will die from this,
not today, not today, but people embrace, touch each other by the wrist
by instinct. The man stands alone, like me, his arms lifted,
perhaps in surrender, perhaps in gratitude.

Between Autumn Equinox
and Winter Solstice, Today

I read a Korean poem
with the line "Today you are the youngest
you will ever be." Today I am the oldest
I have been. Today we drink
buckwheat tea. Today I have heat
in my apartment. Today I think
about the word *chada* in Korean.
It means *cold*. It means *to be filled with*.
It means *to kick*. *To wear*. Today we're worn.
Today you wear the cold. Your chilled skin.
My heart kicks on my skin. Someone said
winter has broken his windows. The heat inside
and the cold outside sent lightning across glass.
Today my heart wears you like curtains. Today
it fills with you. The window in my room
is full of leaves ready to fall. *Chada*, you say. *It's tea*.
We drink. It is cold outside.

Foreigner

you said you counted the ladybugs on our way home;
that you counted exactly twenty; you lifted one off your shirt
and it flew into sparsely leaved branches; you ask me to pronounce
Korean words; *say winter again; say autumn; kyŏul; kaŭl;*
say I sometimes think of you; say it is just so;
you repeat each like a tender bird; ladybugs hibernate in warm houses;
did you know that they're called Asian lady beetles too;
are they transplants like us; ladybugs are only pests by their presence;
I wouldn't harm you either; not even your belongings; next to you
my small mind shivers like some forty wings.

Sometimes when I'm walking on this street

I want to lie down on that patch of dirt and grass.
I'm tired and lonely. On the bus the other day
we passed by an albino tree. You were next to me
and said we need to go back there and look at it,
then flew out the next day. Does white seem cold
or hot to you. We can pretend the tree was full
of ember. On this street are yellow leaves, cool
and aloof. This morning I woke up shivering.
I'd like to tell you of the dream I had, how
I was on a bus to Anmyeondo. I was alone
but you were next to me when we got to the sea.
I'd like to tell you that we found our way
to the island. But I've forgotten everything else.

Easily written poem

After Yun Dong-ju

From the floor of my room in a foreign land. Morning breaks open
with newspapers, each one with terrible promises
of deportation and imprisonment and murder of my friend, a poet,
then another, until they are all gone.
I ran out into the streets though it was not enough.
I screamed out in horror though it was not enough. The sun began
to sink faster, pouring dark over our hair, and I was scared. Still I was selfish—
I found blessed time to write a line lush with songbirds, meteors, and bees,
tuck my notebook under my arm and saunter here, and there, and here.
Meanwhile bombs, drones, and other winged creatures vanished from our sight
and into the living, where we won't find them.
We continue to hum and eat because we can. We sigh and we write
and we read things like this: *a harmless male bee without stingers is called
a drone; it cannot sting to save its own life.*
I lie down. This is the floor. In a foreign land.
This is the vanishing line. This country, here, there, here.
Silly girl. Silly, silly girl for thinking that writing line
after line of beastly beatitudes will help her. How silly,
how silly, silly, silly, silly.

Say Grace

In my country our shamans were women
and our gods multiple until white people brought
an ecstasy of rosaries and our cities today
glow with crosses like graveyards. As a child
in Sunday school I was told I'd go to hell
if I didn't believe in God. Our teacher was a woman
whose daughters wanted to be nuns and I asked,
What about babies and what about Buddha, and she said
They're in hell too and so I memorized prayers
and recited them in front of women
I did not believe in. *Deliver us from evil.*
O sweet virgin Mary, Amen. O sweet. O sweet.
In this country, which calls itself Christian,
what is sweeter than hearing *Have mercy*
on us. From those who serve different gods. O
clement, O loving, O God, O God, amidst ruins,
amidst waters, fleeing, fleeing. *Deliver us from evil.*
O sweet, O sweet. In this country,
point at the moon, at the stars, point at the way the lake lies,
with a hand full of feathers,
and they will look at the feathers. And kill you for it.
If a word for religion they don't believe in is magic,
so be it, let us have magic. Let us have
our own mothers and scarves, our spirits,
our shamans and our sacred books. Let us keep
our stars to ourselves and we shall pray
to no one. Let us eat
what makes us holy.

To the Winter Apricot Blossom

Did I trick you,
with the glow from my window,
the warmth of my skin?

It started with a lone flower,
ember-like in the lifting dusk,
burgeoning on the branch

nosing into my room.
At night the floret shadow dropped
onto my page, my arm, my poem.

In the snow you were heavy
with a hundred bulbs
to light the winter into spring.

A cold misty morning.
You alone illuminate the sky,
small lanterns, red, bursting lobes.

The Transformation

*In early 2016, 13 sperm whales beached themselves
on Germany's North Coast, their stomachs full of plastic litter.*

I was once naive enough to be a woman. I once had a car

silver and new, and drove it over paved roads trilling with rain.

I took it to a pebbled beach lean with ebbing tide, pools of fish

here and there. I could see them, small and lustrous. In deeper waters

were hairtail, and cuttlefish. Hairtail were called knife fish

in my language. If you're shipwrecked, some say,

knife fish are the first to wrap around you

and pick you clean. Silver ribbons sweet

with human meat. But I was no fool. I shed my coat,

my cardigan, my scarf, my hair, and other things of lean beauty.

Rain made my skin stick. I was sickened to my stomach

with the affairs of human concern. Guns and stupidity, mostly:

it was ignorance that hurt us best. Loathing, too, but it is son

to ignorance, a sleek cage. People who love the cage felt snug

and protected. They wheeled it over others, crushing them,

surprising them. I lay in the eerie water. It streamed over me

and other live things, changing us, scale

by scale, strand by strand. It wasn't fair that fish could see color,

and whales could not, but I was okay: I loved my new body.

I don't know what kind of whale I was. In the ocean

there were no mirrors. Pieces of glass and other gleaming debris,

I ate. Hairtail stood like hair and stared at me with their dumb eyes.

A diver once came down to photograph my eyes, then left without showing me

my likeness. I swallowed squid, and their beaks clattered

against the plastic in my stomach. Once I was naive enough to think

to starve with a full stomach meant filling yourself with water.

I then knew that it meant filling my new silver belly with a thousand pieces

of manmade waste. I ate parts from cars just like mine. I ate bags

clear and cloudy, they were blurs to me. Human affairs. How unusual,

how fantastic it feels to be here again, air again, the tide ebbing,

gray sand drying on me—to see a bird fly again, its wing like the belly

of an insect-creature I once saw on the ocean floor,

striped and dead. Look: such slender beauty of things.

Shadows, leaves, rows of clouds pushed

by some animal wind.

Dream Devil

A devil must occupy my dream,
for who else would design
my nightmares, though
they are not truly mine—
I cannot control their cities
nor their rivers full
of bodies.
I clutch your hair
like a drowning person reaching
for floating straw. Maybe it's you—
you keep me from rest. When I speak
Korean with my mother on the phone
my native tongue is a code.
You, a secret.
Still, you form your body
around me, so close that
my dream occupies your dream.
I navigate your sleep,
what you contain is mine—
your sick cats I resurrect
as black lions. Your tormentors:
underwater. I summon bodies, and bodies
of water, and you walk around them
in circles. Like this, we grow old together
without you seeing me.

But morning comes as suddenly
and surely as any morning. You are here,
beside me, fifty years younger—
dear God, I have missed you.
I wait for you to wake.

Time, in Whales

Our legs of yellow skin next to one another,
 calves spread, I think of beached whales, the arcs of their bellies,
 clean and gleaming. A whale would lie in the shape

of something cold, the body sipping on itself
like a drain. Gravity sucks a whole whale onto sand.
 You study Korean, whispering, *murorŭda, murorŭda,*

 meaning, literally, *water rises,* but really meaning, *to improve*
or *to rise in sap,* in springtime trees. Come spring, it will be your birthday.
We will have seaweed soup, supply our blood with oxygen.

 Do you know that Koreans do that, because hundreds of years past,
 they saw whales eating seaweed after giving birth?
 You cross your legs, their hair black and coarse like my father's

and my grandfather's across the ocean. And do you know that whales have hair?
 Perhaps a sign of their past when they walked the earth?
 Summer of years past: your father across the same ocean to bring you

 to America, where you would grow up speaking a language
different from mine. Do you know that whales, too, detect where one another comes from
 through song? That music I hear is yours and ours. *Murorŭda.*

 Murorŭda. Water rises. Whales die in this year's hot winter.
 Your father has told you of the summer, the dank heat.
Your foster mother ran after you, you already asleep in your father's arms,

wailing your name. You will not be called by that name the next day

 and years will pass by. But when you're ten, you will write about that story

 and spell *wail* as the animal, whose breath is a distance, spouting steam,

the great animal that becomes crushed by air and sprayed with words

 Man's Fault. And yes, so perhaps the world will end in water, taking with it

 all loving things. And yes, in grace. Only song, only buoyancy. You rise now

 whispering *murollida, murollida*. Meaning, literally, *to raise water*,

but really meaning *to bring water to a boil*.